I0704747

THE ULTIMATE GUIDE FOR LEARNER DRIVERS

IAN MCQUILLAN

Approved Driving Instructor and
All-round Brilliant Bloke

The Ultimate Guide For Learner Drivers

Ian McQuillan

Copyright © 2022 Ian McQuillan

All rights reserved.

No part of this publication may be reproduced or distributed in print or electronic form without prior permission of the author.

All information contained within this book is intended for educational purposes only.

Contents

Introduction

This book will answer questions and go into detail unlike other books.

My intention is to give you knowledge you would never have access to. I'm giving you 20 years' worth of help and guidance.

My goal is to eradicate mistakes, dispel myths, improve knowledge and boost your confidence.

My aim is to give you the ultimate guide. Once you have reached the end of the book, please tell me if I've improved your knowledge.

Guaranteed improvement is pages away.

Call this a handbook. Call this a quick reference guide. Call this a book of everything you will ever need to become a better driver. Call it whatever you want to call it, but I can promise you one thing, *it will improve your driving.*

Not only will it *improve your driving,* but it will also answer all the questions you have heard from friends, relatives, social media, Roger next door, Billy who apparently passed but the examiner didn't like him and failed him anyway, and Mavis the cat who you tell everything to.

I will do my best to answer questions and queries you have about anything related to learning to drive. If I don't cover them here, feel free to send a message to @drivingadvice on Instagram, Tiktok, Facebook or YouTube and I'll do my best to answer them in a post, reel or video.

I'll discuss things like, 'do you park between 2 cars on your test' and 'you cannot talk to the examiner' and many other things you won't find the answer to unless you speak to an expert. That's me by the way and you now have access to over 20 years of teaching within these pages. And believe me when I say I've SEEN IT ALL and FIXED EVERY-THING - I really have.

This book is not a 'hold your hand' explanation manual or a 'step by step' guide to how to do everything associated with learning to drive. My advice will be given to you much in the same way I teach in real life – with full explanations, relatable content, real life examples and a dash of humour. There will be some things I'll leave to your instructor as it may require a lot of explanation of physical practice that I can't accomplish through words. Use this book to understand why you're making mistakes so you can correct them or prevent them.

One of the main concerns for learner drivers is that they don't want to look stupid by getting things wrong. If I'm being honest here, which you will find is a theme throughout the book, I will tell you EXACTLY what I think when you do something wrong, and you will be very surprised by what I say about it.

To avoid those moments, you have already made the correct decision by reading this book and are well on your way to becoming a better driver. Not only is the information included inside an instant boost to any learner driver, it can also be used in conjunction with your instructor to improve car control, confidence, technique and the chance of you passing your driving test quicker.

If you want to skip all of this jargon and fix your stalling problem or near-death experiences with roundabouts, feel free to jump straight to that section and find out where you've been going wrong. But if you've persevered so far, and I promise to get into the reason why you have made the right choice buying this book, you're already ahead of the millions who will battle on for potentially hundreds of pounds repeating the same mistake and sadly never making it to a driving test.

So well done for using your common sense and hard-earned money to make things easier for yourself, because I admire that kind of thinking and determination to succeed.

While we are on the topic of common sense, you will find me using those two words a lot. Because believe it or not, not using common sense is the main reason why most learners get things wrong. They tend to overthink a situation believing it to be a complex procedure rather than what is the simplest solution. I will be giving you easy techniques to follow and confidence boosting tips in every section.

Lastly, why am I doing all of this for the cost of a coffee? Basically, I want you to enjoy driving and be safe on the road as statistically you are at greater risk of having a fatal accident If you fall into the 17 to 24 age range. Let's not increase those numbers. Instead, you're going to improve quicker than anyone you've ever met because you have everything you need to succeed in the remainder of this book.

Please continue to read on and finally understand why you've been getting things wrong.

If you read every page, and I sincerely hope you do, there will be a link at the end to leave a review. If I've improved your knowledge, and driving, please leave a fab review so others can benefit from this information. I do read every review and I'll thank you personally for your kind words — it is very much appreciated.

<u>Who am I to give advice?</u>

It's a good question. It's *the* question. Here's my answer.

I used to work in an office for seven years before my wife told me about a driving instructor opportunity. I applied for the position purely based on the fact that I loved to drive and was patient (being married taught me that skill), believing those two factors would be the core principles of becoming a decent driving instructor. One half was correct, which was *'loved to drive'* as *'being patient'* is a huge understatement.

Being patient would be something like - asking a friend to pass an Xbox controller, (*YES, I am a gamer*), and they forget to hand it over. Then asking again, for them to look at you, return to playing Skyrim, (*ALAS, a true gamer*) and forgetting to give you your much needed controller. You then ask again with a hint of authority in your voice and a piece of popcorn precisely landing on the end of the nose, resulting in a fist bump for such a skilled throw. However, still not resulting in receiving the controller you stomped over and started an argument which then ended with you hurling the bag of popcorn off their head, and the ignorant friend eating the scattered kernels whilst focusing on battling a Troll with fire and poison axes (*YES indeed, I'm a seasoned gamer*).

Now reading that entire scene took some patience and to be honest, I'm not that accurate with popcorn, but if you managed to read the entire scene without getting bored or thinking about Skyrim, you could be a trainee instructor.

But if you lost your patience with my babbling, you would certainly end up throwing your pupil out of your car whilst on two wheels speeding around the busiest roundabout in your local town.

Now that I've explained my entire working background and hobby, I can tell you why reading this book will change your entire mindset towards learning to drive.

It took me a year and a half to become a driving instructor. During those training sessions I learned one valuable lesson - ***learners are as unpredictable as when a cat will attack your wrists during a belly rub.***

Why are they unpredictable? Because every single person is different. Does that make teaching learners easier? No. Has dealing with unpredictable learners made me a better teacher? Hell yes.

I've encountered a wider selection of skills than you could ever imagine. Ranging from someone who teased a wasp onto his finger, removing it from the vehicle as if it were his pet who followed to his lesson, to someone who took half a decade to learn, including 2 births, 3 house moves, 4 jobs and 5 failed tests. Although, that person wasn't the record for the number of lessons, they did become a very good friend, recommending me to everyone they met during that extra-long period of time.

Having a variety of skills makes teaching fun. I've prevented countless accidents, helped hundreds of people change their lives, and became a local hero, waving numerous times when I drive through my town.

I hope you're getting the picture that I've seen a lot, dealt with even more, and amassed an endless amount of teaching tools over the twenty years.

These techniques, advice, tips, hints and secrets that are about to be revealed in these pages in the simplest (YES, I can do simple) manner for you to understand and put them into practice.

Oh, I've also been teaching since 2002, passed over 500 people, generated 22,250 hours of fixing mistakes, achieved the highest grade possible as a driving instructor, and finally have had nothing but 5 star reviews from the very first person I taught to drive. I really am a modest chap but sometimes you have to explain things so people understand you are vastly experienced and more than qualified to offer advice.

With all those crazy facts thrown at you we can begin with the fun stuff.

Chapter One

WHICH INSTRUCTOR?

If you already have an instructor and you're happy with your progress then feel free to skip this section and move onto chapter 2.

If you haven't selected an instructor yet, continue reading to see how I'd recommend choosing the right one for you.

Ask a friend. THE END.

I could leave it there to be honest but I'll explain why 'asking a friend' is the very best method.

Good old internet

Driving schools usually have a website, Facebook page, and some may have ventured onto social media such as Instagram, TikTok, YouTube and Twitter. Social media serves one purpose only – advertising. It does not in any way explain how the instructor teaches. This is what you should prioritise over popularity with images and shared memes of poor parallel parking and videos of 'mock tests'.

You can select a driving school from google maps or search history when you type in 'Driving schools in Durham' or whatever town/city you live in. I can tell you now, the top school is a paid advert. The second one is a paid advert too, and so is the third one.

This certainly doesn't give a good indication of the instructor or the school as paid adverts are usually done by large driving schools. I will explain the difference between a large driving school and independent driving schools.

So now you are scrolling down google search looking for a driving school that has a website or Facebook page which has managed to make it to the first or second page of Google. Firstly, well done to those instructors getting their page noticed, but it still doesn't indicate the teaching qualities of an instructor.

We all read reviews before we buy something, so why don't we look at driving school reviews to see what the instructor is like? You can, but it still doesn't indicate a level of teaching and what the instructor is like. The reason being is that a review is usually left by someone who has just passed their driving test. This will always result in a positive review and therefore 5 stars. Although it is a good indication of what the instructor is like, it doesn't fully describe how good they are.

You have narrowed it down to not fully trusting the internet to find out what the instructor is like, which leaves asking friends and family who they would recommend.

Family

They will always recommend the oldest instructor they know because the older generation strongly believe in the value of a moral code. This is loosely translated to "go with Jim, he's been doing it since our Steven passed," - who is now married with four kids and has no hair.

Jim may well have been a family friend and Jack may indeed have no hair, but unless Jim is familiar with modern techniques and not continuing with old teaching methods, he won't be the best person to push you forwards or understand how times have changed. And trust me, the older instructors don't like change. I've met a lot and they sadly have the 'I teach the way I teach' method.

This brings us to the difference between large driving schools and an independent one. We've ruled out Jim due to old techniques, replacing him with someone who is experienced, yet works hard to maintain a good standard of teaching to keep their reputation as positive as possible.

A large driving school supplies the instructor with a steady stream of pupils, meaning they don't have to achieve the highest level of reputation as they will receive new pupils if they discard any. Sadly, this can be the case with some.

An independent instructor will do everything in their power to give you the best of their ability. Why? Because their reputation depends on recommendations from their students. They don't rely on advertising because, as mentioned before, the bigger schools paid adverts will nearly always be selected first. If they do a good job the pupil will tell their friends how much they enjoy their lessons, ultimately passing and raving about how good their instructor was.

The large driving school will have some good instructors working for them, but you cannot be certain which instructor you will receive as they supply you with the one who has free time to take you on. And I'm saying this now, if someone has plenty of free time, they won't have a better reputation than the keen independent who is trying their best to give you the best service possible.

A good instructor never has free time because their reputation is always being passed around through word of mouth.

An instructor with plenty of free time has the opposite.

I've been teaching for 20 years and never had to advertise.

So how does this translate to asking a friend?

Your friends will tell you this:

How patient the instructor is. How reliable they are. How punctual they are. How funny they are (crucial on most days). How up to date they are with modern techniques such as sat nav and independent driving. How they explain things such as manoeuvres. How much they charge. How helpful they were during pre-test and test. How flexible they were. How calming they were. How easy they are to get along with. And lastly, how nice the car was.

To summarise: this can simply be – "They are great."

Or, if you ask enough questions, you can get the answers listed above. Please don't read out the list of questions and make them answer each one. They are your friends after all - ***trust them***.

You simply cannot gain this level of insight anywhere else. And if the instructor isn't best suited to you – you can always blame your friend.

Chapter Two

WHAT TO EXPECT FROM YOUR INSTRUCTOR

Now you have chosen your instructor, this is what you should expect. BRILLIANCE.

Although, BRILLIANCE is only reserved for my level of teaching, this is what should happen before, during, and at the end of each lesson.

The first question an instructor should ask you is, "Hello Captain Crabstick, how's your crew and what's the name of your parrot?" translated to, "How's things?"

This is my first question because it will dictate the structure of the lesson.

If I get a, "I had a late night, or 'my head is battered, obviously not recently dipped in crispy goodness, but stating they have things on their mind," then I reevaluate the intended lesson plan to something less challenging.

Whatever I hear will inevitably be followed up with further questions to determine how they are mentally. Physically is always fine unless they really have come out with a head looking like a chicken nugget. Driving is a lot of mental processing and I need to know how much concentration my pupil can muster during their lesson.

FYI, if you're any of the above, tell your instructor. They will/should change the level of difficulty to match your state of mind. I know what you're saying, "I'll lose momentum and not improve if the level of difficulty is reduced for the lesson". Not at all. Your instructor can focus on manoeuvres or a lesson plan that focuses on technique rather than forward planning.

A lesson plan is the first conversation after determining 'level of focus'.

A lesson plan should include a goal that can be achieved by the end of the lesson. I will add that lesson goals can change depending on other faults that may require priority action.

The lesson plan should fit in with your learning curve and push your driving skill enough to improve it by the end of the driving lesson.

Important: You will usually only improve a small amount each lesson. A small amount is the ideal level of improvement.

Your lesson should begin with a goal you intend to achieve which isn't always achieved due to the level of complexity/difficulty.

During the lesson, don't get disheartened if you don't achieve the goal by the middle of the lesson. It really does take repetition for certain skills to be absorbed. Persevere with what your instructor is teaching you and wait until the end to see improvement. This is where patience is needed by you and your instructor. Some subjects have to be repeated numerous times to be fully understood. This is normal practice.

The end should include a de-brief. This is where you discuss your intended goal and to see if you've achieved the goal. If you have – WELL DONE. If you haven't, continue the same lesson plan on your next lesson and be proud you gave it everything you had.

***Note: This is an overall outline of a driving lesson and not EXACTLY how it should be done. Every instructor has their own technique and as long as you improve you are doing everything right, as is the instructor.**

Chapter Three

TEACHING QUALITIES

Is it important for your instructor to be experienced?

If you say no, please close the book and pop to Halfords to purchase a bike.

If you say yes, I'm happy you agree with me.

Experience is everything

I learned this after approximately five years of teaching. The more experience you have as an instructor the more tools you have to fix mistakes. After all, learning to drive is about making mistakes and allowing your instructor to correct them by utilizing what we in the trade call 'knowledge transfer'.

The more knowledge an instructor has the quicker, and easier, they will improve your driving. You would be astonished at the amount of tools and tricks I could draw upon to fix ANY issue you may have.

I will give you one example that will probably frighten you when I say it but by the end you will understand the importance and reason for it.

Here we go, strap in, buckle up, hang on, hold your breath, and don't repeat this with your mam and dad.

When a pupil can't steer. AKA 'shit man, we nearly ran over Morris, and 1993 flashed before my eyes twice in the last five minutes,' I will then proceed to remove one hand from the steering wheel, usually the left hand, and place it on the gearstick - to remain there until I say otherwise.

FYI If you can't steer and are left-handed, prepare for a week of nightmares and possible therapy.

The usual response I get is, "I'm petrified. Are you mad? Are you joking? Tell my parents I love them," while sweat trickles down their heads. Luckily, my pupils know my level of tuition and trust my methods.

At first it is a bit sketchy. AKA "Bloody hell, one of my ears has gone and I've lost the ability to speak," but after a few minutes something remarkable happens – my ear grows back OR steering improves.

How is this possible for someone who couldn't possibly control a vehicle with two hands to suddenly gain the ability to steer WITH ONLY ONE HAND?

How – *like **HOW**?*

Because, when both hands are on the wheel, a learner will primarily depend on the left hand to do everything. It changes gear, puts the indicator on, fidgets in ears and nose, and is basically the hero hand. This means the right hand becomes lazy and when the left hand is doing one of the aforementioned the right hand does absolutely nothing.

That's right, ABSOLUTELY NOTHING, remaining on the top of the steering wheel like a hot dog. I have been known to label such a lazy limb as a hot dog, only promoting it to a sausage when steering improves.

When the left hand is removed the right hand HAS to steer. It has no choice. And believe me, it steers because the will to survive is usually important.

When the left hand is eventually replaced you will have learned that when turning right, the dominant hand is the right and vice versa for turning left. This exersize forces the brain to adopt those principles and instantly improves steering. Previously, both hands attempted to steer in both directions creating uncertainty when turning.

This brings us back to **experience is everything.**

This kind of knowledge only comes from experience and a good dash of bravery. Other techniques can be applied to other faults, but if experience isn't there, things like poor steering will only improve over time through pure determination and a touch of fear.

An experienced instructor is the *perfect instructor*. They can fix mistakes in one conversation.

Without going into further dramatics, I'll add that an instructor who has helped a variety of individuals will be better skilled to help you and your oddities.

Chapter Four

How many more lessons do I need before I can go for my test?

I get asked this at least once by every single pupil I've met – equating to over 5,000 times.

My answer: NONE – GET OUT FOR ASKING SUCH AN IMPOSSIBLE QUESTION.

Okay, the real answer is: Depends on how quick you pick things up.

That answer covers every possible scenario and ends the conversation without giving an actual amount, because it really is impossible to give an exact number.

I've had pupils pass in less than ten hours and several that have taken years.

Learning how to drive is possibly the hardest thing you will ever do. That is not an exaggeration. If you are used to multi-tasking, moving every limb, eyes, and brain in different directions – often at speed, then you will be in the lower range of lessons. If not, you will fall into the average amount. If you struggle with any of the suggestions above, you will be in the higher range of lessons.

But seeing as though you're reading this section, I will give some figures.

1. Less than 20 hours if you have some form of road experience, such as a motorbike, farm vehicles or a misspent youth.
2. Between 20 to 30 if you pick things up rapidly and have regular lessons to instill learned behaviour.
3. Between 30 to 40 if you learn at a steady pace and pick things up quickly while progressing through each lesson understanding the topic, improving at the end of every lesson.
4. Over 40 if you ask how many lessons you will need OR anyone who struggles with roundabouts, because they are the hardest and scariest thing to learn and teach.
5. Forever if you have the coordination of a carrot.

These are guidelines and it is possible to see a surge of skill if you have a burst of awesomeness and decide to scare your mam, dad, or friends with how you can steer with one hand.

BEGINNER LESSONS

Lessons 0 - 10

Expectation vs Reality

What should you expect within the first 5 to 10 hours versus what is the REALITY of what will happen in the first 5 to 10 hours.

Expectation of what you *believe* will happen is very different to what will *actually* happen. You will receive a lot of new information during the first 10 hours which is a lot to comprehend, let alone perfect. That is the simple answer. Please let me explain.

Assuming you are a novice and have never had any form of experience driving before, you will enter the driver seat for the first time full of anxiety, sweat, an inability to speak, washing machine stomach and full limb failure. I've named it: ***First Failure Syndrome.***

How long does that medical condition last? Until you stop worrying about crashing and dying. There, I've said it and now we can move on with understanding more and you can finally remove the fear associated with First Failure Syndrome, abbreviated to FFS. (You sighed; I know.)

Why are the first few lessons so terrifying?

The answer is a mixture of – friends, relatives, social media, self-doubt.

If you spoke to a driving instructor about how your first few lessons would go then you'd have far less FFS.

I hope, after reading this book, your FFS will have been reduced. If so, please tell me how it went via one of my social media platforms listed at the end of the book.

Friends - DO THEY HELP?

You will have some friends that enjoy making you feel scared. Comments like, "I'll stay off the road. Good luck, you'll need it," doesn't help ease your nerves. Even knowing it's not possible or practical for them to do what they're saying, it doesn't stop them saying it numerous times. Plus, they were scared on their first lesson and sadly they want you to feel what they felt.

Social Media DOES IT HELP?

There are literally millions of memes, videos, stories and whatever else, about learner drivers being horrendously bad. How many have you stumbled across that made you feel less confident about your first lesson? The reason being: failure is funny. People have made millions from getting things wrong. You've Been Framed started off the trend of laughing at people's failures. Social media rewards people for posting videos of failures; including learner drivers.

Relatives DO THEY HELP?

These are you best bet for reducing nerves because they are more likely to reassure you that you will be fine because they don't want you coming back to them in tears after suffering a bad dose of FFS. They will say things like, "You'll be fine. Just do your best. We've all been there."

These all feed into your psyche and fill it with trepidation, fear, anxiety and FFS.

Let me tip the balance in your favour

Imagine I was your friend. Heck, you pretty much are now that you've read a lot about my past. So, as we are practically friends, please read the next section as many times as you want. I promise it will reduce FFS.

When you have your first lesson I will explain everything to you, and I'll repeat it as many times as needed so you'll know EXACTLY what you're about to do. If something doesn't quite make sense to you, I will REPEAT it as many times as you need or say it a DIFFERENT way until you understand it.

I will show you with my pedals how to use the clutch. I will explain PRECISELY how to use it and let you practice as many times as you need until you're comfortable with it.

When you move away, you will only go 5mph to 10mph MAXIMUM until YOU are ready to go faster. That may be in 5 minutes or 5 months. Whenever that time comes, you will be ready to progress.

I will help you with your steering, making it IMPOSSIBLE to hit the kerb.

When you need to stop the car, I will tell you EXACTLY what to do, because I don't want to visit A & E with whiplash. Trust me, the worst part for me is how hard you brake on the very first attempt. I will MAKE SURE you are very gentle with the brake - it's in OUR best interest.

When you stop, I will TELL YOU to keep your feet still so you can take it out of gear and apply the handbrake. After all of that has been done, THEN you can look over to me and tell me how GOOD it felt to drive a car.

We will do it TOGETHER.

Notice how I said 'TOGETHER'. This is the one word you've probably never considered, but as a friend I can assure you we will progress through your learning TOGETHER.

The one thing that will reduce your nerves INSTANTLY is the fact that you and I will do the first lesson together. You certainly won't be left to battle through FFS, scaring Jean as she tries to dive into the bushes, dragging her dog Poppy in with her.

Think of it this way

Let's pretend for a moment that you take a flying lesson. Yes, I'm aware this is designed to reduce nerves, and if you're anything like me you'll hate heights and never ever attempt to fly a plane, but it works perfectly for this example.

When the pilot says, "Okay, you have control of the airplane," do you really think for one minute you have the capability of plummeting the darn thing to mother earth by pushing some stick forward and letting your neck snap back while you swallow your own vomit? I've painted a lovely picture there. You're very welcome.

I'm assuming you said the pilot would take over the controls before you crash landed in the cereal aisle of Tesco's. He would - every single time.

I am THAT same pilot, I just don't have a fancy hat and a silver badge that looks remarkably like the golden snitch.

If ANYTHING were to happen during your first lesson I WOULD TAKE CONTROL of the car.

If you don't think that's possible because I'm old and you're not, you've underestimated the power of experience. Remember how many times I've seen people make mistakes. I'm like a meerkat ready to strike the millisecond you THINK about doing something wrong.

Quite often pupils have said to me, "How did you know I was going to do that?" and I reply, "Because I'm a psychic and have special powers," which gets a laugh and is way better than saying the truth, "I've seen it happen at least a hundred thousand times."

SUMMARISE

Your first lesson will be explained fully and you won't do anything on your own unless you're fully capable. You should be directed every step of the way and have the entire process explained as often as you need. At no point will you do anything wrong that will affect others because if your instructor is anything like me (a driving Jedi), you will be TOTALLY FINE.

Now that you know nothing bad can happen and every-thing will be made crystal clear, how nervous will you be?

I'm guessing a lot less than before and if this hasn't helped one bit, wear a crash helmet and a nappy.

One more note

Please don't worry about looking stupid for making mistakes. I've seen every single mistake you're worrying about and have dealt with them more times that I care to imagine. I expect mistakes and you *will* do them. It's natural to get things wrong. Accept that. It's fine. Just don't shit yourself.

Expectation

Worrying about having an accident. Not wanting to look stupid. Mutilating Jean and Poppy. Scaring passers-by. Having some kind of panic attack. Possible bowl eviction.

Reality

The instructor has everything under control.

Chapter Six

CAR CONTROLS AND NOT STALLING

Lessons 0 - 10

In this chapter I will discuss controlling the vehicle and give you tips to make each element easier to understand and operate.

Before I give you my expert advice, I will start by saying the hardest thing to learn is not the clutch, not changing gears, not moving away or stopping. STEERING is by far the most difficult thing to master. Surprised to read that? Then you'll be pleased to know that 90% of my pupils reacted the same way when it told them they will struggle with it.

Moving away without stalling - wooohooo

It's best practice to do this with the engine off. After all, it's a brand-new subject and there will be a lot of information to absorb, so it will feel easier with the engine off to practice moving away.

Here we go. How to move the car away **without stalling** every single time:

Put your clutch down and move the gearstick into 1st.

Bring your clutch up SLOWLY. When I say SLOWLY, what I actually mean is SO PAINSTAKINGLY SLOWLY THAT WE COULD COUNT TO 5 BEFORE IT COMES ALL THE WAY UP. Sorry for SHOUTING, but everyone's 'slow' is different. Ask you instructor to help you with the correct speed by using the dual control pedal to slow you down to the required speed. Once you've got the correct speed, then you're ready to try with the engine on.

Do EXACTLY the same thing and the car WILL MOVE. YOU DO NOT NEED POWER. This will teach you how to use the clutch correctly without revving the engine so hard you smell it burning.

I will include 'adding in power' later in the book. For now, bring it up slowly until you get a feel for how the car responds when the clutch comes up – which is called the 'bite'.

Different instructors will use different methods, such as adding in power, handbrake on and off, holding the clutch for a second and some say keep your foot on the brake. Whatever tuition they use MAKE SURE your clutch comes up EXACTLY the same time, i.e. SLOWLY and if you get it spot on and the vehicle doesn't stall – repeat it FOREVER.

You will only stall if you bring your clutch up too quickly. Learning to move away is all about repetition. If it works, don't change it, no matter how confident you get.

When you master the speed of the clutch then you add in the power. This will allow you to move away at speed AFTER the car is moving. It is IMPOSSIBLE to stall the vehicle if it is already moving.

SUMMARISE

Clutch up super slowly until the car moves – repeat – never ever quicker

IMPROVEMENT TIP

Take notice how high the clutch is when the car starts to move. Make sure your clutch is at its slowest during that time and you will never ever stall.

CONFIDENCE BOOSTER

Try doing this five times in a row without stalling. If you can do that, you have understood and learned how to use the clutch. WELL DONE.

Chapter Seven

CAR CONTROLS AND STEERING

Lessons 0 - 10

I'll start with a simple instruction here - DON'T DO THE DEATH GRIP.

I know you're fearing for your life and Jean is hoping you will have FULL CONTROL of the car that is hurtling towards her at 2mph, but believe me, strangling the wheel won't help in the slightest, and will in fact make it near impossible to steer.

It's the same as being on a rollercoaster, also known as driving lessons on a country road with a pupil who suddenly believes as if they're playing Forza is how you tackle dangerous corners and hidden dips. If you're not that bad you will more than likely grip onto the wheel with a vice like grip thinking it will help. Nope. Not one bit. Have you ever seen someone grip the bars of a ride and say, "Ahhh, I'm not petrified anymore. Let me put my hands in the air and smile for the camera." The reality is that you will hang onto the wheel believing if you let go it will do a scene from Harry Potter and fly away into some poor family or a nearby garden.

What should you do?

Let go of the bloody wheel. Loosen your grip. Smile through gritted teeth and wave at Jean.

When you grip the wheel it creates anxiety which in turn feeds fear. Hold the wheel like you would hold a toddler's hand. If you don't have access to a toddler, imagine being a zoo keeper and you had to walk a monkey around the zoo, knowing fine well it loves nothing better than to hurl its own shit at folk.

There we go, much better. Oh, and the instructor is there to avoid knocking Jean and her stick into a farmer's field. He will keep you safe unless he has his eyes covered, then good luck my friend, take Jean for a bonnet ride she'll never forget.

SUMMARISE

Relax your arms and loosen your grip.

IMPROVEMENT TIP

Keep your hands as high as possible on the wheel. Aim your hands where you want to go and the car will follow.

CONFIDENCE BOOSTER

Try letting go of the wheel. You'll be surprised what happens.

Chapter Eight

CAR CONTROLS AND GEARS

Lessons 0 - 10

Gears

If you believed changing gears would be the hardest part, you've been fed poor advice from someone who clearly hates you or drives an automatic.

They are very easy to understand and master. Once you've done it the first time, it is just repetition after that.

The easiest way to understand gears and when to change them is:

1st Gear $0 - 10$ mph

2nd Gear $10 - 20$ mph

3rd Gear $20 - 30$ mph

4th Gear $30 - 40$ mph

5th Gear $40 - 50$ mph

6th Gear 50 – 88 mph Please get the *Back to the Future* reference and do not aim for 88mph.

You will be using 1st, 2nd, 3rd, during the first few 0 to 5 lessons.

Your instructor should be asking you to go up and down gears. The same principle applies when you slow down. Reduce speed - reduce the gear.

This concept applies for the rest of your lessons and onwards unless you want to learn in a dodgem car (automatic). I'm not against learning in one but considering how gears are not that difficult to learn, it really is a shame that once you pass in one you have to do another test to drive a manual car.

How to change gear.

Stay off the power during the gear change. It's normal for the speed to reduce during the change.

When you have finished putting the gear into its correct place, then bring the clutch back up. REMEMBER to bring it up the same speed you did when pulling the car away – SMOOTHLY AND CONSTANTLY. Once you have completed the gear change, then put your foot back on the power.

This is simple advice for how to change gear correctly. As you progress through your lessons you will add power as the clutch is coming up. I will add this into the **Advanced** section of the book.

SUMMARISE

Every 10 miles per hour will require the next gear. Keep off the accelerator and keep the clutch down while you change the gear until you are more confident with changing gear.

IMPROVEMENT TIP

Try to do the gear change without looking. If you manage to locate and select the correct gear – WELL DONE.

CONFIDENCE BOOSTER

If you managed to change gear without too many mistakes, you're ready to move onto the next stage of driving.

Chapter Nine

CAR CONTROLS AND STOPPING THE VEHICLE

Lessons 0 - 10

Stopping

Bringing the car to a smooth stop depends solely on how focused you are with your brake, and not being afraid to 'increase or decrease' pressure on the pedal.

Once you're moving and have avoided Jean, you will need to stop the vehicle. Don't worry about trying to get close to the kerb, that will come with more practice.

On your first lesson, please don't try to park really close to the kerb and accidentally plough through the fields shouting, "yeeee haaaa," because the price of your driving lessons may suddenly increase.

Get as close as you think is close (which won't be close), and stop the car. Make sure you come off the accelerator (obvious, I know, but you'd be surprised how many people don't) and apply pressure to the brake.

As the car slows put the CLUTCH all the way to the floor. This can be done as hard and as fast as you want. Not the brake by the way, seeing your instructors eyeballs stretch out of his head will not be forgotten.

When the clutch is down, you may then bring the car to a gentle stop.

This next bit of advice is crucial for the well-being of your spine and will make your instructor super happy and impressed with your skills. DON'T PRESS THE BRAKE HARDER while the car is coming to a stop. If it is slowing down, maintain the same pressure on the brake and it will eventually roll to a smooth stop.

Think about the last time you were on a bicycle. When you want to stop a bicycle, you never pull the brakes hard - EVER. You apply them gently until it stops because you don't want to Superman over the handlebars. The same logic applies to a car. After all, it's on wheels just the same as a bicycle.

When you have come to a complete stop – KEEP YOUR FEET STILL.

This isn't a time to do a line dance in celebration, save that for when you get out of the car, announcing to your fans you never stalled.

SUMMARISE

Gentle braking. Keep clutch and brake down whilst coming to a stop. Remove feet (not literally) from the pedals.

IMPROVEMENT TIP

If you are braking too harshly and too soon, release the amount of pressure you have on the brake.

CONFIDENCE BOOSTER

Stopping gently means you have mastered stopping. Onto the next phase. Bravo.

Chapter Ten

ROAD POSITION

Lessons 0 - 10

In this chapter I will discuss road position and give you tips to make each element easier to understand and use.

Before I give you my expert advice, I will start by saying road position is possibly the easiest part you will do in the first 0 – 10 lessons. This can be the first opportunity for you to enjoy driving. If not, therapy can be cheap if you block book.

At this point you should be able to move away and stop the car with a reasonable amount of accuracy. If not, please continue with the previous lessons until you gain the confidence to tackle the main roads.

The good news is that this part of driving may seem more difficult as you are ON THE MAIN ROADS..*GULP, but this is easier than everything you've done so far. Let me explain.

All you have to do is keep the vehicle in the center part of your lane, go faster and do more gears – at speed.

Wait, I'm not doing a great job of selling this 'easier' section, am I? How about I tell you all you have to do is 1 more gear and keep the vehicle in the same place. Does that help? If it does, the next part is a breeze. If that seems like a task you don't feel ready to tackle, please do more practice and return back here when you're ready to frighten the general public.

Road position

If you can stop looking at your speedometer for long enough to keep yourself in between the white lines and the kerb, you deserve a biscuit. Not the cheap kind. I'm thinking of a chocolate delight, a king of snacks and a worthy reward – choc chip cookie. This will be handed to you with a cup of tea, or a glass of milk, if you can maintain correct road position for a good few minutes or miles.

The trick to keeping your vehicle in the correct location is to NOT STARE AT YOUR SPEED. By all means, look at it occasionally to make sure you're not speeding. BUT, priority is keeping you and your proud instructor alive. It doesn't matter what speed you were doing if you're milking cows from a half open window while parked in its dining room.

To help maintain a consistent road position, try to put your vehicle over the dark line you can see in the middle of your lane. If you look ahead you will see it, it's the section other cars don't touch, and by the way, neither should you.

Another way to keep a correct road position is to look in your door mirrors. This will take a modicum of skill but the effort is worth it.

You should see equal distance between the white lines and the kerb if you look at the left and right door mirrors. DON'T STARE.

There's a logical reason for the car to veer away from the middle of the road. This is known as 'your hands follow your eyes', which means when you look away, your hands move in the same direction, taking the vehicle with it.

Your main focus should be the road ahead, but from experience (and I have more than most), that isn't enough. I've seen pupils look ahead and drive into an oncoming car, a parked car, a dog, a blindman, a postman, a horse, a POLICE OFFICER, a lollipop person, a cyclist, a runner, a tractor, a friend, a parent.

Try to get an understanding for where your vehicle is by looking at the road ahead, confirming it with the mirrors, and even looking around if you dare. If you managed to maintain correct road position you are doing BRILLIANT and should be very proud right now. If you find this difficult, keep doing this until it becomes easier. It can be quite daunting at first but after a few attempts it gets easier.

SUMMARISE

Keep your eyes on the road ahead. Use whatever you can to keep the car in the center of the lane. Don't stare at anything unless it's an ice cream van announcing a sale.

IMPROVEMENT TIP

Relax. Follow the road with your hands. Brake early and take your time.

CONFIDENCE BOOSTER

If you can drive near the speed limit AND maintain road position, you are 100% ready for the next level. Congratulations for completing the BASICS. If you done this within 10 hours, you're a natural. I'm proud of you.

Chapter Eleven

JUNCTIONS

Lessons 0 - 10

In this chapter I will discuss dealing with junctions and give you tips that may make each element easier to understand and navigate.

Before I give you my expert advice, I will start by saying junctions may seem easy at first but they can be very difficult and create a lot of nerves if not done correctly. Just as well I'm going to make it easy for you then.

T Junctions.

Left and right turns are the only junctions you should be dealing with in the first ten lessons. The reason is because you will be dealing with crossing the path of oncoming cars. This is quite scary at first and can lead to a lot of anxiety.

I'm going to explain turning left at T junctions then turning left into a side road before I go into detail about right turns. The reason for this is because crossing traffic can be difficult to do if done first and lead to possible learner evacuation and the dreaded FFS.

T junction LEFT - Open and Closed Junctions

Always approach in second gear.

An **open** junction is when your view is unrestricted in both directions. This means it is possible to follow the road around to the left whilst keeping in 2nd gear.

This will require some assistance by your instructor if you still find steering difficult.

A **closed** junction is when your visibility is reduced. This means you will need to stop at the give way lines because it may not be clear for you to exit.

Again, your instructor may help you with the steering element. Move away when no one is coming and don't be a hero and think your learner car can 'formula one' it out of there by flooring the accelerator. All that will do is give your instructor heart palpitations and force local residents to call the POLICE believing the car has been stolen.

LEFT turns from a main road to a side road

No matter how fast you were travelling before the left-hand turn, make sure you're doing approximately 15 – 17 mph BEFORE you get to the turn. This speed coincides with 2nd gear. The speed and gear HAS to be done BEFORE you get to the junction. If you don't manage to get the speed and gear done before the junction, prepare for words of wisdom from your instructor, possibly resulting in FFS for you BOTH.

T junction right

Keep to the right-hand side as close to the white lines as possible and keep both eyes open. The only difference here is when you merge from the junction you have to make sure both sides of the road are clear before emerging, saying "peekaboo," as you move out from the give way lines. Try your best to steer, keeping the vehicle on the correct side of the road. That's the left. We haven't time-warped to Benidorm, ready to cruise the sunny delights, admiring the uneven tans and lucky lucky men. Keep to the left.

You may need some assistance from your instructor, who may be dreaming of buying a dodgy watch from said 'lucky lucky men – Asda price', while avoiding a near death experience as your multitasking has reached its limit.

RIGHT turns from a main road to a side road

Not the same as left. Not in the slightest. The 2nd gear and 15 -17 mph is the same and to be done BEFORE you get anywhere near the turn. Don't be afraid to do the speed and gear WELL IN ADVANCE of the turn. No one has had early retirement from doing things early. Early is fine at this stage in your learning. If you see a vehicle coming towards you in the opposite direction, hopefully on their side of the road - STOP before you reach the turn. Again, early is fine. Stopping late will result in action from your instructor and possible swear words from all involved. Once stopped, move away when clear and try to turn into the junction, keeping on your side of the road. It may sound easy, but keeping between the kerb and the centre line, while moving into the new road is very difficult. If you get this right – **BRAVO**, book your test.

SUMMARISE

Left turns – follow kerb. 2nd gear if the road is clear. Right turns – SPEED AND GEAR done early. STOP if an oncoming car prevents the turn.

IMPROVEMENT TIP

Do your speed and gear early. This will help with steering into the junction.

CONFIDENCE BOOSTER

Focus on one thing at a time. Keep the car slow on approach. Position and gears will feel a lot easier and lead to quick progress. If you find junctions difficult, that is the norm. If you tackle these with ease – ask for a fist bump, that is very rare. Not the fist bump, the skill to tackle and overcome junctions.

Chapter Twelve

PROGRESS AFTER 10 LESSONS

If you're reading this chapter, you're ready to tackle the harder stuff. I'm very proud you've made it this far. Not only have you demonstrated being super skillful with your driving, you've proved that reading a book can be enjoyable if done with a hint of humour, (I say hint because even my child rolls her eyes at my attempt at humour), and yet you made it this far. The best is yet to come.

Keep up with your lessons, and keep turning the pages as you're about to delve into the best part about driving – other road users.

Assuming you've had approximately ten lessons you should be well versed in going up and down gears, including 1st to 2nd, to 3rd, to 4th. Don't worry about 5th gear for the time being. That will come when you're confident in your ability at changing gear, and not looking at the gear above 40mph. For now, using 1,2,3,4 is enough to turn you into a proper driver.

Your road position should be at a level where you can keep your car, ALMOST central and have a good concept of speed, and go up and down gears without too many mistakes.

Mistakes are fine at this stage. You should still find difficulty in slowing down, changing gear and maintaining road position. This will improve over time and nothing you should be overly concerned with at this stage in your learning.

If you're confident with speeding up, changing gears, slowing down and coming down your gears, then you are ready to be part of the general traffic.

If you're not confident with keeping up with other cars, doing junctions the same as others, and afraid of moving away, maintain this level of tuition until it becomes easier.

SUMMARISE

After 10 lessons you should be able to handle your vehicle with a certain level of confidence.

IMPROVEMENT TIP

Don't stress about the cars behind you. Focus on your braking and coming back down gears.

CONFIDENCE BOOSTER

You've been attempting a VERY DIFFICULT stage in driving – THE BEGINNING . Moving away, changing gears, keeping up with other traffic, AND making sure your road position is reasonably accurate, IS EXTREMELY GOOD. You have my admiration and I can happily say – "You got this."

Chapter Thirteen

INTERMEDIATE LESSONS

Improvement and progress

What improvement should you expect within the next 10 to 20 hours?

First of all, well done for understanding how a car works, using those skills to navigate junctions and tackle the scary prospect of dealing with other motorists. There's an old saying that your parents or grandparents might say at some point in your learning. It goes something like this:

"It's not you I'm worried about, it's everybody else."

We've all been subjected to that saying at one point in your learning from a friend or family member, but I can assure you it's very much YOU I'm worried about at this new stage and NOBODY ELSE.

For an instructor, letting a new pupil loose on the main roads to tackle things like roundabouts, more roundabouts, even harder roundabouts, and those complex round things with lights on that make you wait and question why simple math and lane choices are suddenly the worlds hardest puzzle, possibly re-igniting FFS, while inching a way around a roundabout, expecting another car to ruin you life.

Apart from those cement M&M's, everything else is a breeze. Oh, and mini roundabouts, let the fun and games commence, also known as 'entering Squid Game' for the nervous and weak willed.

But don't worry, I've got your back, front, side, inside, outside, side-side and I've been saving my Jedi mind force to restrain cars who want to rugby tackle us. But considering how complex roundabouts can be, I'll be giving them their own special chapter.

This is where experience comes in. Remember how important it was for an instructor to have a good amount of years dealing with learner mistakes? What that really means, is how brave the instructor is and how much of a gambler the learner chooses to be. I'll explain all when we discuss roundabouts and you'll be beyond surprised when I explain the mindset of a learner at roundabouts.

Chapter Fourteen

MIRRORS AND USE OF MIRRORS

Mirrors

I'll start with mirrors because without these little reflections of goodness, nothing else would be possible.

Note: I usually introduce mirrors during the junction phase but each instructor will have their own timing when to incorporate them. I will use them here as their use is much more important with regards to general public on and off the roads, rather than talking about them for junctions and repeating myself here.

I'm going to explain this what the examiners expect from you and your mirror use.

The short version is that if the examiner notices the hazard before you, they will look at you to see if you have noticed the hazard.

In simple form. You see the hazard and look behind to see if it's safe to slow down. The examiner watches all of this and is mightily impressed.

I will summarise mirrors rather than giving hundreds of examples.

Mirror Use

Look in a mirror BEFORE you move the car. The specific mirror depends on the direction of the car. Speeding up and slowing down is the rear-view mirror. Left door mirror before turning left and right door mirror before turning right. Include looking in side mirrors when you have a lane either side of you.

If a vehicle is behind you, or alongside you, consider your actions before applying the brake or accelerator.

Your instructor will go into detail in regards to these actions and should include who and what to look for in your mirrors.

Chapter Fifteen

PEDESTRIAN CROSSINGS

You don't need to apply specific highway code rules for every type of crossing you encounter. The reason for that is because you've probably forgotten.

The main thing you need to know about dealing with pedestrian crossings is to slow down (looking in the rear-view mirror first) when you see someone approaching them. If they are brave, they will start to cross. And they really don't care if you've seen them or not, they EXPECT you to see them and STOP. This is very much correct, but places a great deal of responsibility at your inexperienced feet.

To keep things simple, look for people near crossings and slow down. Stop if you think they may cross. It is fine to stop even if the person doesn't cross, teasing you with some kind of Irish jig before walking away, much to your frustration, and your instructor's.

Chapter Sixteen

CROSSROADS

Box Junctions

These painted puzzles are feared by all road users, except by driving instructors. The crazy thing is that all the confusion stems from one statement. And to give the millions of road users some credit, the statement in question could be made simpler. This is the culprit:

Highway Code Rule 174

You MUST NOT enter the box until your exit road or lane is clear. However, you may enter the box and wait when you want to turn right, and are only stopped from doing so by oncoming traffic, or by other vehicles waiting to turn right.

Lovely and non-complicated, isn't it? Let me K.I.S.S. for you.

Only enter a box junction if your exit is clear. The 'exit' is the road you intend to drive into, continuing your journey.

Don't get in if you can't get out – is my *simple* simple version.

Your instructor will add things like nearside to nearside, offside to offside and when to go, enter, wait and leave, for every type of box junction you encounter.

Chapter Seventeen

CARRIAGEWAYS

Single and Dual Carriageways

It's quite surprising that you may encounter these as soon as you start driving on the main roads. The speed limits for both are not a target and only to be reached if you've had extensive rally driver experience, done stunt driving, and have been playing GTA for at least five years.

Single carriageway speed limit is 60

Dual carriageway speed limit is 70

The easy way to remember the speed limits is that the extra lane (i.e. dual meaning two), has an extra 10 mph.

Travelling at speed can be scary and dangerous for everyone involved on the carriageway. Only go on these roads when your car handling, gear changing, lane discipline and life insurance is at the correct level. Discuss joining and leaving and defensive driving with your instructor. I'm sure they will ignore you entirely and suggest doing something less dangerous.

Chapter Eighteen

PLANNING AHEAD

Forward Planning

I can't begin to explain how important forward planning is for a learner driver. Luckily for you, I will.

Here are some similar concepts applied to multi-million-pound industries.

Fail to prepare – prepare to fail OR Poor preparation leads to poor performance.

Without planning ahead, you will 100% fail to deal with it correctly. To enhance this concept, I usually read out a chapter which used to be handed out to pupils who failed their driving test so they could identify their error and correct it before returning for another driving test.

*You must be aware of other road users at all times. Your examiner is looking to see that you plan ahead to judge what other road users are going to do. This will allow you to predict how their actions will affect you and **react in good time**. You needed to anticipate road* *and traffic conditions, and act in good time,* **rather than reacting to them at the last moment.**

The way to understand, and relate to forward planning, is how you use it in everyday life. And the descriptions I'm going to use will highlight the importance of learning from mistakes and my exceptional storytelling capabilities.

Scene 1 *Going out*

You've been asked to go out for food and drinks and you need to be ready by 7pm. Simple. I'm also assuming you're not the type to rock up at 8pm announcing you are fashionably late. Here we go.

You think about your outfit for days before, maybe purchasing something new, looking at it often as you pass its location. On the day, you time the bath/shower in advance so you have enough time to apply make-up/shave, leaving enough time to put on your new outfit, admiring yourself numerous times, telling yourself how good you look and feel. Then you will run through a check list of items. Keys. Money. Phone. Making sure you have every item ready BEFORE you wait for 7pm to arrive.

YOU CERTAINLY WILL NOT mix up that routine, leave it super close to the deadline, rushing your make up and forgetting your mobile phone. There's very little chance you would do that, and in the off chance you were late upon starting these events you will constantly remind yourself what needs to be done as the time nears 7pm.

That is forward planning.

· · ·

Scene 2 *Making Sunday dinner*

Assuming you're old enough to understand the importance of a Yorkshire pudding, then this explanation will highlight how well you forward plan. If not, don't invite me around for Sunday dinner.

The oven always goes on early and if it's the chaos that is Christmas Day, then it will be switched on seconds after 'the big man' has demolished his treats and headed into the clouds behind panting reindeers due to scoffing marks and sparks finest minced meat, which always confuses me by the way. Having sweet meat, in a shell-like dome, that resembles a steak pie, gives me the Turkish Delight vibes. Anyways, back to Sunday dinner and the timing of the oven is done with military precision so to not overheat the kitchen and to be at the correct temperature for a bird with four limbs, and whoever eats the neck has my heartfelt appreciation, but not welcome to join me in a buffet.

Vegetables are peeled, prepped – which is basically putting them in a pan, then left to look at the extractor fan while the bird gets its own liquified insides, which reminds me of how I sweat when doing any activity, poured back over its naked skin. Is it skin? It is isn't it. All of this is done to precise timing, often guided by the 'round clock' in the kitchen, and hardly ever the timer on the front of the oven.

I'm still going, hang in there.

The table is set when the food begins to make its way to the rest of the house, telling everyone food and crackers are about to be tossed around the room, and no doubt one of the relatives will spill a glass of wine.

They will all be directed to the seating area, which has been placed with exacting standards that could win some kind of award. Food is then marched from the kitchen, arms stretched out, followed by – "Careful everyone," Or in my house, "where's the cat." He is called Ninja for a very good reason and has a penchant for chicken.

Everyone sits down and remains in the invisible straight jacket, while the red faced sweat creature tells everyone how hard 'that was' and follows it with some kind of poem behind closed eyes (probably still stinging from opening and closing the oven doors enough to cause chicken blindess.)

All done and ready to eat at exactly the time the food preparer stated.

Impressive? Absolutely.

Now you have some, rather detailed, examples of how we all do forward planning. Yes, you do it to. And to anyone who doubts they have the ability to forward plan anything, have you ever made a cup of tea or coffee? Don't you put the kettle on first? Then grab the cup? Why don't you grab the cup first? Because forward planning has taught you to do things a certain way to save time and energy.

How can we apply all this pre-learned knowledge to driving?

Here's the answer.

DON'T LEAVE THINGS TO THE LAST SECOND.

There we go, all covered.

But before I move on, I will give a little of my knowledge for how good forward planning can be. No harm ever comes from doing anything early. Nothing. NOT A

THING. Many things, bad things, come from leaving things a second too late. Let that sink in.

One more note

Please don't worry about affecting the cars behind, they are expecting you to brake early.

IMPROVEMENT TIP

As soon as you see a hazard ahead, look behind, then apply your brake. This will give you time to change gear(s) and process what is ahead.

CONFIDENCE BOOSTER

Keep doing this and in time driving will become very easy, very quickly.

Chapter Nineteen

PARALLEL PARK

The Problem

As a category, manoeuvrers are the most complicated things to learn.

Every single learner fears them and tells me they are worried about doing them, and this is before they have put the gear in reverse.

How on earth is this possible if they have never tried it before?

There is a logical answer and what I'm about to explain will more than likely leave you gobsmacked.

Society as a whole, including your friends and parents, will tell you reversing is hard. Social media adds to this universal problem, instilling that reversing a car is extremely difficult to do, AS IT WAS FOR *THEM*.

AS IT WAS FOR THEM for them is the problem. I will now give you the answer as to why reversing a car was indeed difficult for them.

It was hard because they were taught a way that was difficult to understand, complete under pressure, and not applicable to when they passed their test and bought their first car.

With this being the case, it is fully understandable why reversing was extremely difficult for them to grasp. This then results in them never attempting to reverse, which compounds the problem even more.

I will clear up things a little here. This is a problem stemming from the Parallel Park.

The 'three point' turn never created any reversing issues. When your parents, or older, all they had to do was put it in reverse and steer the opposite way. There was very little thought process involved to leave a long-lasting problem. It was a simple, steer this way then the other way, etc

The left reverse around a corner was also a manoeuvre in the past. This did require a level of skill that was needed to follow a kerb using whatever method they chose. It was part of the reversing problem, but sadly the evil that is known as the Parallel Park took the first prize, leaving the left reverse picking up second place in the 'I hate manoeuvres' declaration.

If you don't believe me, ask your parents or grandparents which manoeuver they hated the most.

But why is this such a problem? Who is at fault?

The simple answer: The Driving Instructor.

Not me of course, but the vast majority of driving instructors have instilled a learned behaviour which is incorrect. And if any driving instructors are reading this, please read on before announcing I don't know what I'm talking about – because I do.

Driving Instructors are given a syllabus to teach. This includes how to teach the Parallel Park. It also included the left reverse and the three-point turn, but because they are no longer taught I will focus on the Parallel Park for reference.

The protocol for instructors is to teach a method. This method is called the 121. I will explain this soon. They are then assessed by an examiner to see if they meet the driving standards level of teaching before they can qualify as an Approved Driving Instructor.

One of the assessments is teaching the Parallel Park. Therefore, the driving instructor has to teach the 121 method to pass the exam to become a fully qualified driving instructor.

The 121 method is:
1 Full turn to the left
2 Full turns to the right
1 Full turn back to the left

This method has been taught to all pupils by all instructors and has created a multitude of problems. This is where the reversing problem comes from.

The turns are applied in opposite directions. This has to be done to complete the manoeuvre correctly. But WHEN are the 121 turns done?

We've found the evil critter that is the root of all reversing hatred. It lives in the mind of all learners who try to figure out reversing in opposite directions when looking behind. Even typing this leaves me wanting to delete it all in fear of confusing you.

But *it is* the problem.

The Parallel Park lesson continues for weeks, leaving the poor learner fearing the dreaded manoeuvre for weeks at a time, often leaving them with anxiety wondering if they will be asked to perform it on the driving test.

Driving instructors try to fix the problem with repetition. *The sign of insanity is doing the same thing expecting a different result.*

The learner driver will learn the basic concept of a Parallel Park BUT it will never be fully learned and mastered because the 1 2 1 technique is only applicable to the instructor's car and it has to follow a strict set of learned guidelines to give the learner a vague understanding. Things like learning reference points, stickers on cars and homework have been used to reinforce a routine. That in itself tells me that it is over complicated. Add in pressure of a driving test, which usually results in forgetting refer-ence points, then the chance of following a complex routine whilst under the scrutiny of an examiner, and the possibility of another car being impatient, is a HUGE PROBLEM – often resulting in a fail, therefore enforcing the hatred of the dreaded Parallel Park.

If the learner passes, with or without performing the Parallel Park, they will be left with a muddled routine that can only be applied to the instructor's car. This results in a fear of doing it in 'real life' with added worry of damaging their own car and someone else's.

Can you see why the nation has such a hatred of the Parallel Park? Quite rightly so.

Is there a fix to this mess? Absolutely, and what I'm about to say will shock you and hopefully give any driving instructors a different insight into teaching this 'supposedly difficult' manoeuvre.

Here we go:

Parallel Parking is EXACTLY the same as parking forwards.

Mind blown? It is hard to believe, but it is the exact same routine as driving towards the kerb and parking up. Let me prove this.

Parking forwards

Head towards the kerb. Move away when you're getting close. Steer back towards the kerb. Straighten up.

Parallel Park

Head towards the kerb. Move away when you're getting close. Steer back towards the kerb. Straighten up. Yes, I copied and pasted. Yes, it's correct. Yes, I'm a hero and will rid the world of Parallel Park problems.

I know you're going to say, "But you need to get in between 2 cars." No, you don't. That is a myth.

I know you're going to say, "I need to get in close behind the car, which is different to parking forwards." No, you don't. That is a myth.

I know you're going to say, "I need to follow the routine my instructor taught me or I'll fail." No, you don't. That is a myth.

I know you're going to say, "Oh my goodness. I can't believe no one has ever told me this before. I must go out and buy Ian McQuillan some Lego, fluffy slippers and a new set of golf clubs." No, you don't. The set of golf clubs will be enough. Ta.

So, if the 121 method doesn't work, why do the Driving Standards Agency and the driving examiners expect you to follow it? They don't. That's a myth too. I haven't taught that routine in 15 years. It took me 5 years to realise that method had huge implications and I therefore changed it to how I preferred to teach it.

How do I teach the Parallel Park you may ask.

Simple.

Look in the left door mirror and head towards the kerb, (same as forwards) then move away from the kerb when you think you're getting close, (same as forwards), then if you're too close or too far away feel free to adjust your steering towards or away from the kerb, (same as forwards), then straighten up once the kerb is parallel to the car, (same as forwards).

I never use the word OPPOSITE. It can create so many problems, especially when you're using a mirror. I always say closer to the kerb or further away from the kerb. This is a very simple technique to remember and follow while under pressure.

I can say FOR CERTAIN that my learners all learn the Parallel Park in less than 1 hour. They all drive home wondering why all their friends say it's difficult.

Remember the K.I.S.S. abbreviation? It very much applies to the Parallel Park.

Parallel Park problem resolved? Absolutely.

During the manoeuvre, make sure you look around CONSTANTLY. You need to be aware of hazards ALL AROUND your vehicle at all times. The trick to achieving this is to look around non-stop. It is fine to look in your door mirror to reverse. I know this because I've been teaching this for 15 years and have not had a single enquiry from a driving examiner about the teaching method.

Why don't the Driving Standards Agency tell instructors to teach this way?

The answer is because they are worried you will stare in your mirror and miss hazards approaching your car. Don't prove them right by staring at them. Look around CONSTANTLY.

Now you understand reversing is the same steering as forwards, this steering technique (towards the kerb or away from the kerb,) applies to the bay park reverse and the pull up on the right and reverse back for 2 car lengths.

One more note

It is fine to correct a mistake whilst doing a manoeuvre. The examiners like to see corrections, it's the sign of experience.

IMPROVEMENT TIP

Practice doing full lock at the beginning of the manoeuvre to see how quickly the car approaches the kerb and practice moving it away quickly to compensate.

CONFIDENCE BOOSTER

If this seems too good to be true, feel free to ask over 500 learners of mine who will tell you the exact same thing. It's easy once you know the easy method. And just for clarity, ask anyone who can Parallel Park (parents or friends) if they use the 121 method. You'll find they don't.

If you've made it here, I've got to admit something.

To prove how serious I am/was in showing the world this simple life hack, I dressed up in a super hero outfit and reversed around cars recording the manoeuvre and its simplicity. Then I created a website to give it away for free. I was known as The Reverser and had a cracking yellow and black outfit. Sadly, due to the huge file sizes, bearing in mind this was before TikTok and IG video/reels, the video detailing it all was too large to download. But I thoroughly enjoyed doing them and dressing up as a superhero was one of the most amazing experiences I've ever had.

Chapter Twenty

ROUNDABOUTS

And here we are. The impossible task of helping you overcome your fear of roundabouts. Is it possible to give a healthy amount of information that will improve understanding and confidence towards roundabouts? Absolutely, so let's get started.

DON'T DO IT.

This will make more sense as you continue reading through my wisdom, and advice, of all things roundaboutish.

The most important element of roundabouts is knowing when to enter the roundabout. This sounds easy in theory but in reality, it's very difficult. There are many factors at play for this to be done successfully.

I'll list them for you to understand your struggle isn't without reason.

1. Lack of confidence in moving the car away
2. Not certain where the cars are going
3. Not sure where your destination is

4. Worried about being hesitant
5. Concerned about the car behind
6. Unsure if a car is leaving the roundabout
7. Confused at seeing a car with no indicator
8. Scared if you get it wrong you may be in an accident
9. Confused if there are a number of cars to figure out
10. Not trusting other drivers

There we go, 10 reasons why roundabouts are the hardest thing to learn, and quite rightly so.

I've explained to hundreds of pupils that learning to drive takes approximately 8 months. During that period, it takes approximately 1 month to learn the basics of driving, i.e. stop, start, gears and steering. It then takes the remaining 7 months to be confident in dealing with roundabouts. That says it all.

I could list all 10 issues and explain how to overcome them, but I won't as discussing each issue in detail can actually do more harm than good. What I will do instead, is make your decision making a whole lot easier for you, which in turn will make roundabouts a lot easier to deal with.

Before you tackle any roundabouts, make sure you can move the car away with confidence. This is essential. If you lack skill at moving the car away at will, try this exersize.

Ask your instructor to count you down from 3. When they get to 1 you should've moved the car away from a stationary position. If it takes you longer than 3 seconds, repeat until you move the car away before your instructor gets to 1. Ideally, you should move the car away before you get to 2. That is the level of skill you need before tackling circles of doom.

Once you've gained racing driver level of moving away, your confidence 'to go' when the gap is there won't cause you any concern. That is crucial.

Let's just say you're there and ready to move away but unsure when to go. Let's discuss that next.

To put it simply, you can 'go' if no one is driving TOWARDS you.

Or

You CAN'T GO, if someone IS HEADING TOWARDS YOU.

This is a simple concept that learners over complicate. No matter how many cars are on the damn thing, if no one is HEADING TOWARDS YOU – GO.

Is that too simple to understand? Not at all. In fact, it may seem too easy a concept to follow. The good news is that it is exactly what you should do. Add in the ability to move your car away with ease, this could fix your roundabout problems forever.

This is the point where you should add power when you want to move away. I've mentioned earlier that you will need to add power to move the car away, and now is that time.

If you really hate roundabouts, and they appear in your nightmares, along with Voldermort, Parallel Parking and having an interview, then read on.

99% of driver indicators on a roundabout are correct – trust them.

However, for the idiotic 1% who are on the roads who don't believe in telling people where they are going on roundabouts, then DOUBLE CHECK they are going where you believe they are going.

The DOUBLE CHECK part of driving will save your life. Yes. I'm saying that because I've saved lives from doing exactly that – every single day. If I DON'T do the double check procedure, I'm then hoping that all cars do what they say they are doing – which in 1% IS NOT the case.

If a car isn't indicating at all, they are going ahead from wherever they came from, just the same way you don't indicate when you are going straight ahead. They do exactly the same because if they indicated left or right, they would be in an accident at some point. So, when you see a car with no indicator, unless they are the 1%, they are going straight ahead. Trust this.

Trust me. I've been doing this longer than you've been alive.

What would be ideal is for the driver to signal his intention to leave the roundabout, point at where they are going, have a blimp attached to the roof with a massive arrow showing they are leaving the roundabout, a set of Forza like arrows showing exactly where they are drifting, and finally a set of dancing roundabout clowns, pointing at you while screaming, "Go, Go, Go," making it eventually safe for you to move away. If anyone ever invents this game, I'll have the royalty payments in bars of chocolate – ta.

But all you get, if you're lucky, is an indicator done at the correct time to state their intention. That IS ALL YOU GET my friend. That is your sign to move away like you stole the car.

If you wait until they leave, confirming your suspicions, then be prepared to be there until the moon arrives and clown shadows appear, and NO ONE wants that image.

At first you won't trust anyone, but to pass your test you need to demonstrate you trust your fellow drivers. It won't be done on your first lesson for the reasons 1 to 10 listed above, but if you can remember to move away quickly when the opportunity is there, you will gain confidence in roundabouts very quickly, and that's a very good thing to have.

If YOU ARE UNSURE exactly what they are doing, DON'T move away. **Don't do it.**

Don't do it. I told you this would make sense now. A Geordie lad said something that I use regularly as a teaching aid when a learner is uncertain when to 'go' at a roundabout.

It went *If in doubt – dee nowt.*

Please practice your Geordie accent, and fingers crossed it doesn't sound Scottish.

This little saying is an excellent way to figure out if you should or shouldn't move away, and this is why it should ALWAYS be applied to roundabouts.

If you think there is a gap 'to go' but you're uncertain what the other drivers are doing, your brain has already processed everything you're seeing and made the decision for you. **Don't do it.** Because if it was clear to 'go' you wouldn't have any doubt at all. So, if you have doubt, it's there for a reason. If in doubt – dee nowt.

You should now have more clarity when it comes to decision making with roundabouts. You should have more confidence knowing when to 'go' and you should appreciate my bravery and foresight in dealing with not only the 1%, but the **FFS** that might suddenly appear when you see the circles of doom.

Every roundabout is individual. But because of the inconsistent traffic flow, complex lane markings, volume of traffic, and variety of roundabout exits, I can't go into exact details as it would take too long and it wouldn't cover every scenario – sadly. All of this should be discussed and detailed by your instructor. Good luck, and never be afraid to ask for things to be repeated.

My advice would be to pick a route of three to four roundabouts. Keep going around that route until they become easy.

I have a 'nursery route' (technical term), I keep my pupils on until they get used to gears, lanes, observations and indication. It is easier if you stick to the same roundabouts until your experience grows.

IMPROVEMENT TIP

Approach roundabouts between 15mph and 17mph. This will give you enough time to work out what other drivers are doing.

CONFIDENCE BOOSTER

Make sure you take note of the roundabout sign. It has all the information needed to perfect the circles of doom. Once you've mastered roundabouts, you're ready to go for your driving test.

Chapter Twenty-One

ADVANCED LESSONS

Improvement and progress

What improvement should you expect within the final lessons leading up to your test? You should have completed approximately 30 to 40 hours and have a sound understanding of junctions, roundabouts and manoeuvres.

Now the real driving begins – independent driving.

So far you have accomplished a lot. Some of those tasks will have had some help or guidance from your instructor, which is normal and best practice. The real question is, how much have you ACTUALLY learned and how much of your experience so far has been supported by your instructor?

The only way to find out what you've learned so far is to try to put it ALL into practice on your own and not relying on your driving instructor. The best way to do this is to drive entirely on your own by following signs or sat nav directions.

Which is easier– following signs or sat nav direction?

Sat nav direction is much easier and only has one real problem that you will have to figure out yourself. That problem is figuring out which lane to use, including indicators, if necessary, when you arrive at a roundabout. This is because a sat nav will only say 1st, 2nd, 3rd, 4th etc exit. You will need to work out exactly where the exit is and what lane to use, including indicators. That's all. Not difficult at all - *gulp.

Next is following signs. If you've been following signs up to this point then happy days, you've already got some experience under your (seat) belt. But doing things on your own, i.e. independent driving is far harder, requiring extensive knowledge of road markings, layout, lane choices and discipline.

The good news is that if you can manage independent driving by following signs there is nothing left to learn. You are officially the same as other drivers, apart from the years of experience and cheap insurance they all have.

Include test routes in your independent driving. This is the time to drive around the harder roads. You should be ready to tackle anything in front of you at this point. If new roads scare you still, keep doing independent driving until you don't fear junctions or roundabouts you haven't seen before.

Also, include mock tests as part of your independent driving.

I vary my mock tests, offering a different level of difficulty and pressure, easing you into the lonely world of pretending to be on a real test. By the way, mock tests are used to prepare you for driving in silence. They don't actually prepare you for the real driving test. That is a whole different beast I will discuss in a later chapter.

Try these mock tests:

1. Numbered Mock Test
2. See how many minutes you can drive before making 15 minor mistakes. Aim for at least 30 minutes. Focus as hard as you can and ignore errors.

1. Error Mock Test
2. Ask your instructor to only point out errors, including reason and solution for 40 minutes. This will prepare you to ignore your mistakes and not dwell on them which will inevitably lead to more mistakes.

1. Real Mock Test
2. Start outside of the car. Do the vehicle maintenance questions before driving. Then follow your instructor's guidance. Try to do things entirely on your own. Aim for less than 15 minors and 3 serious mistakes.

Some of these mock tests may be new for your instructor. If so, ask them to try them with you. I've designed them to build up confidence, to not dwell on mistakes, prepare you for driving on your own and to get you used to concentrating for the entire duration.

One more note

I have a check list of all the difficult areas included within the test routes. I give a copy to every pupil and tick each one as we complete them. Some have to be done numerous times due to the level of difficulty.

Ask your instructor to do something similar or ask to go around the hardest places on your test routes until you are fairly familiar with them. If you want more of a test, do them without any help from your instructor.

IMPROVEMENT TIP

You will make mistakes at first. That is normal progression. Better to get all of the mistakes out of the way, rather than on your driving test. Learn from them and don't be afraid to ask for full explanations for each one. Knowledge is power.

CONFIDENCE BOOSTER

If you can drive without any assistance or very little from your instructor then you are ready for your driving test. Remember, you are allowed mistakes so try not to aim for perfection. Give yourself a little bit of leeway as this will reduce pressure.

Chapter Twenty-Two

DRIVING TEST

Well done, you've made it here and also pushed through all the difficult challenges that were put before you on each lesson.

Statistically speaking, you're one of the few who start driving lessons and continue all the way to the driving test.

But before we get you over the final hurdle, let's increase the odds of you passing your test.

I'm going to start with a quiz.

1. What is the most common reason for a learner failing their driving test?
2. Hesitation
3. Parallel Park – don't let that be you after reading this book
4. Forward planning
5. Nerves

The answer is all of them if you never read this book before the test, or option d.

I'll let you into a secret about the driving examiners.

They have already passed you before you start the test, it's up to you to fail. And they are very nice people. Please don't be offended if they don't talk to you. They are either scared speechless or thinking about what directions to give you. They certainly don't hate you or want you to fail. The reason is that failing a driving test will include a serious error. Trust me, they'd much prefer to be driven around the test route without experiencing something that will result in a failure.

How can we reduce nerves and increase your chances of passing? The answer is down to applying a different mental approach. Can you do this? Absolutely. Let me explain:

I'm going to use school subjects as an example so you can relate to it easier.

Math Exam and an English Exam

Many apologies for taking you back to school or college if you've escaped and hated Math and English but it's the best example to use.

Math Exam Example

You have a Math exam coming up soon. You love Math and I mean lovvvvve Math. It will be your career because you love all the complexities and puzzles that come from numbers. You have a perfect job or university placement waiting on your expected perfect exam score. The thought of being involved in Math for the rest of your life makes you happy – beyond belief.

With your entire future relying on you passing, how nervous will you be? I'd say VERY. And rightly so because your whole life and career relies on you passing the exam.

Math Exam - VERY NERVOUS

You have an English exam coming up soon. You hate English and I mean haaaaate English. It will never be your career because you don't get comma's, despise Shakespeare and prefer to live life to its fullest rather than spend time reading books (obviously, apart from this one). You have a perfect job or university placement doing something other than English. The thought of being involved in anything related to English makes you unhappy – terribly sad.

With all these things relying on you passing, how nervous will you be? I'd say NOT VERY. And rightly so because your whole life DOES NOT rely on you passing the exam.

English Exam - NOT VERY NERVOUS

You attend both exams because your parents and teachers would go crazy if you didn't go.

You **passed** them both.

One made you physically sick, gave you numerous sleepless nights while the other one didn't give you an ounce of worry.

How will knowing this help you pass your driving test?

Approach your driving test as if it were the English Exam.

You need to convince yourself it doesn't matter if you fail.

Yes, I know, before you say IT DOES matter, of course it does but look at what nerves do to a driving test. Nerves are the reason the majority of learners FAIL.

Convince yourself by saying it doesn't really matter, and that you can have another go (which you can by the way), and your nerves will reduce, increasing your chances of passing.

I have explained this logic to many nervous pupils with a very high success rate.

If you say, "I won't drive very well because I won't care," I've got you covered.

Of course, you'll drive well, do you WANT TO FAIL?

Preparing your mind for failure doesn't mean failure, it means an increased chance of passing due to the lower levels of stress during the driving test, which in turn means you drive the way you do on your driving lessons.

Is there any other way to reduce driving test nerves? Yes.

1. Drive for enough hours that any difficulty you encounter is very easy for you to deal with
2. Turn a pan upside down
3. Eat a banana
4. Carry a lucky charm

Option 1 is the only one that works but I've experienced all the others, including a woman in labour while driving around the test route.

You can apply the same approach to driving lessons to reduce anxiety. It doesn't matter if you don't do well on

EVERY lesson. It's fine to get things wrong. It's okay to sweat. Just remember it's not okay to shit yourself.

One more note

Be confident – not arrogant.

IMPROVEMENT TIP

Focus on every hazard in front of you and don't dwell on your mistakes.

CONFIDENCE BOOSTER

If your driving instructor has confidence in your driving ability and say's "you should pass," believe them. It's when they say, "please bring the car back on 4 wheels with 2 mirrors," when you need to rethink your driving test date.

Chapter Twenty-Three

WHEN YOU PASS

I'm proud, and yet wondering why you're reading this book after already passing your driving test. I'm certainly not complaining and I will always be grateful for anyone who has taken time to read my book.

So, what do you do now? Ask your parents or friends for their car keys and tell them you're off to London for a drive out. Good luck with that.

Which car should you get? How often should you drive?

If you have a car, or can purchase one soon after your driving test, try and drive it as soon as possible.

Spend some time getting familiar with the most important thing – the radio. After that, find where the bite is and practice moving the car away. It won't take very long to find out what makes the car stall. Once you're comfortable with the new vehicle, head out for a drive on a quiet road and brake early when you approach your first hazard.

Try and get in and out of your car as often as possible. This will feel strange at first, especially if you're on your own. After a few days your new car will become easier to drive and your confidence will improve.

Don't be afraid to ask for more driving lessons if you are still nervous behind the wheel. Or ask your instructor to help you get familiar with your new pride and joy. I'm certain it will be better than my first car. When I pressed the clutch and brake together all the pedals came loose and fell down. Luckily, I didn't have it long, but I absolutely loved the little crap coloured death trap. My second car liked to turn itself off when I turned a corner. Thankfully, I survived all those, and many more near death experiences to give you all these nuggets of wisdom.

Chapter Twenty-Four

IF YOU DON'T PASS

It's fine to cry.

I failed four times and look at me now, writing a book and avoiding going to work.

I remember, very clearly, when I failed my first driving test. I said goodbye to my driving instructor, (who was my third one because the first two were apparently too scared), and ran upstairs to cry into my pillow.

Stupidly, I'd left my driving licence in the car and he knocked on my door a few moments later.

I answered not knowing who it was. He saw my tear-soaked face and said, "It's all good mate, let it out. See you next week."

Eight months later I returned to driving lessons. It took me approximately five lessons to get to the same standard I was when I failed. Then I needed another ten to remember all the things I'd been taught eight months previous.

Don't do what I did.

Return to your lessons as soon as possible and get more practice in. In addition, practice everything and not just what you failed on. It is very rare you will fail with the same mistake. Improve as much as you can and your chances of passing will dramatically increase as you have a lot of experience under your belt when you do the next one.

Remember, experience is key.

Book another driving test as soon as you can. This will be your motivation and help you remain focused until the new driving test date.

To help pass your test, read this book again.

A Final Few Words

Firstly, I'd like to say thank you for purchasing the book and making it to the end.

When I started writing this book, I wanted to give you as much of my knowledge as possible. I couldn't go into as much detail as I'd normally do on a driving lesson, but if this book was enjoyable to read and you've learned something new, or even fixed any driving mistakes, I'd love to know about what worked for you. If you want to leave feedback or ask further questions about your driving test or driving lessons, please use the social media accounts below OR leave a review on Amazon.

I fully intend to write more books to help you pass your driving test and to make driving lessons enjoyable. To keep updated with any new releases, feel free to follow me across my social media accounts where I will be posting videos and giving more hints and tips.

Website: www.ianmcquillan.co.uk

See you there and thank you for your review.

Ian

facebook.com/IanMcQuillanDrivingSchool

instagram.com/ianmcquillandriving

tiktok.com/@ianmcquillandriving

www.ingramcontent.com/pod-product-compliance
Lightning Source LLC
Chambersburg PA
CBHW061245250726
48653CB00002B/519